Title Page

77 Seconds to Sales Success

*The Practical, Tactical, No-Fluff Guide
to Excelling as a Salesperson*

By

Kenneth G. Hasty

Edited by

Kate Hinz

i

Copyright Page

Dedication

77 Seconds to Sales Success *is dedicated in loving memory to my role model, my mentor, and one of the best salesmen who ever lived, my father, Lawrence G. Hasty.*

Introduction

It seems like every time I train a salesperson, he or she tells me I should write a book to help salespeople in general. That is why I wrote *77 Seconds to Sales Success*, the practical, tactical, no-fluff guide to excelling as a salesperson. This book is designed to benefit you in every phase of your sales career.

These days, nobody wants to read a sales encyclopedia or a novel on sales. The premise of *77 Seconds to Sales Success* is that each of the 52 chapters only takes about 77 seconds to read.

Research shows that most people read approximately 300 words per minute. The body of each chapter is roughly 385 words, which would take about 77 seconds to read at 300 words per minute.

I wrote this book in a conversational tone as if I was working directly with you at the time. In some chapters I used stories from my past experiences to illuminate key points and to show you what has worked for me.

You can read and apply one chapter per week for a year or read the entire book in a little over an hour — or both.

Either way, I suggest you keep it handy as a quick reference guide to help you excel as a salesperson.

Happy selling,

Kenneth G. Hasty

Table of Contents

Title Page..i

Copyright Page ii

Dedication iii

Introduction iv

PRACTICAL ADVICE AND GUIDANCE...............................0

    Treat Everyone You Meet With Respect..........................1

    Ask if You Can Ask...4

    What You Say and How You Say It................................7

    Love What You Do 10

    Why Use a CRM?..13

    Using Multimedia...17

    Pick Up the Phone and Call.....................................20

    Ongoing Sales...24

    Office Software 27

    Think for Them..30

    Be Ready for Anything...33

    Plan in Advance for Events......................................36

    Remind Your Manners...39

    Understanding Your Bosses.....................................42

    When It Hits the Fan 45

    What's In It for Me?..48

    Don't Bring Your Baggage.......................................51

    Following Company Policies 54

Working With Your Peers.. 57

BEFORE YOUR SALES CALL... 60

The Internet Changed Everything 61

Researching Your Prospective Customer....................... 64

What to Bring 67

Getting There... 70

You Only Get One Chance to Make a First Impression . 73

Rehearse Your Elevator Pitch................................... 76

Walking In.. 79

Know Your Competition... 82

Motivating Yourself... 85

Reaching "C"-Level Executives.................................. 88

SELLING.. 92

Hasty Sales Presentation....................................... 93

Key Account Management... 97

Loading Your Gun 101

Feel Selling 104

Getting and Using Referrals 107

Farmers, Hunters and Apex Predators 110

Selling to Different Personalities 114

Selling Over the Telephone 118

Selling to Doctors 122

Selling to Engineering Specifications 125

Selling Capital Equipment 128

Selling Through Dealers 131

Meeting with "C"-Level Executives 135

Selling to "C"-Level Executives 139

When and How to Follow Up 143

CLOSING..146

Bite-Sized Pieces 147

Benefit Closing 150

If You Were Me 153

Some Closing Techniques 156

Overcoming Objections 159

GETTING YOUR NEXT JOB IN SALES................................163

Your Resume for a Sales Job..164

Interviewing for a Sales Job...168

Moving Up the Ladder 172

Acknowledgements vi

About the Author.. viii

PRACTICAL ADVICE AND GUIDANCE

Treat Everyone You Meet With Respect

Years ago, I had a job as a warehouseman. Oftentimes, salespeople would come through my part of the building to get to the office personnel. This gave me a great way to observe how sales representatives approach their potential customers.

Most of the sales representatives would completely ignore me, ask me for directions to someone's office, or ask me who to speak with about their product or service.

Sometimes the sales representatives would bring donuts. I could see them walking in from the parking lot and, well, I like donuts. So I would politely steer them in the right direction in hopes that they would reward me with a donut, which they usually did not.

In fact, some of them were so impersonal to me that I felt like they barely even regarded me as a fellow human being.

The few really good salespeople (at least from my perspective at the time) would offer me a donut or two as they came through my area. I looked forward to their visits.

When we had our company meetings, management would ask my opinion about the various products and services they were considering. I think you can guess which ones I preferred to recommend if they fit our needs.

In an interesting twist of fate, I was promoted to a position that included being responsible for purchasing. I definitely favored the sales representatives who were nice to me in my previous position.

I never forgot those early lessons I learned by observing salespeople from my little corner of the warehouse.

One year, a company relocated me and I had to prospect an entirely new sales territory. I made it a regular practice to bring plenty of morning donuts or afternoon cookies for my potential customers as well as their entire staffs.

Sometimes this meant bringing as many as six dozen donuts. I would tape my business cards to each box so the entire place would know who was taking care of them. Some of their staffs affectionately called me "the cookie man."

I also earned the award for "salesman of the year" that year.

When soliciting a new prospective customer, be sure to treat everyone kindly and with respect. Any person you encounter could be a family member of the boss, or even the next purchasing agent.

"Never look down on anybody unless you're helping them up."
Jesse Jackson

Ask if You Can Ask

As we go about our workdays, we often have to ask strangers for directions. Some people are naturally friendly and will offer to help you if you look lost or otherwise confused about something. That said, many people have no desire to help you or answer any of your questions. They are the stoic people who are good at simply ignoring your presence.

Let's say you are trying to find Main Street in a busy city. You are not likely to get much help from these individuals if you use questions like, "Hey, buddy, how do I get to Main Street?" or whistle and say, "Hey, pal, where's Main Street?" In fact, they might even send you the wrong way on purpose!

In my travels, I have learned to simply "ask if I can ask" them a question. I greet them politely and acknowledge them as individuals, saying something like this: "Excuse me. Could I ask you a quick question?" They almost always respond favorably with a yes, sure, or something to that effect. Then I would say, "Could you please tell me how to get to Main Street from here?" They tell me, I thank them, and we have had a nice, pleasant interaction.

In sales, I have found a variation of "ask if you can ask" to be very helpful when cold-calling. We have all cold-called an office where the receptionist is about as friendly as a pet rock and has been kicking salespeople out all day. She totally ignores you when you walk up and is quick to curtly tell you that they are too busy to see salespeople.

Something magic often happens when I humbly approach these individuals like this: "Hi, could I ask you a favor?" This totally changes the game, and now they cautiously say something like, "What kind of favor?"

The next words out of your mouth will make or break your opportunity to get to the next level. I might say something like: "I see you are very busy and I obviously don't have an appointment, but I was hoping you could tell me who I could speak with about my product."

Now you have a conversation going that can lead to the next step, such as the buyer's name, an appointment or maybe even an introduction!

"Though I speak with the tongues of men and of angels, but have not love, I have become sounding brass or a clanging cymbal."

1 Corinthians 13:1

What You Say and How You Say It

One of the great things about being a salesperson is that you can say whatever you want to say, however you want to say it. This gives you a lot of leeway in how you present your products and services.

Years ago, as a young outside salesperson, I was making some telemarketing phone calls from the regional office. We were lucky to have an outstanding regional manager, William N. Reese. He taught me something that changed my selling style, in a good way, for the remainder of my career. He had been listening to my telemarketing pitch on the phone. Then he walked up behind me, slapped me on the back, jumped back, and said, "Get animated, Ken!"

Ever since that day, my sales presentations have been enthusiastic and animated. Enthusiasm is a powerful sales tool. Think about how little kids get enthusiastic when they want to convince you to take them somewhere or buy them something. It works.

How you say things can make all the difference in how your message is received. Southern belles have a unique way of saying anything they want about anybody without being too offensive. In their sweet southern accents, they can be brutally honest as long as they finish with something like, "Bless her little heart."

They can look you square in the eye and say, "You are just so full of yourself; bless your little heart." They make their point, and somehow you walk away without feeling offended. I love working in the South. In fact, I am writing this book from the French Quarter of New Orleans.

The words you use are important. I try to avoid absolutes such as "always" and "never" unless I mean them, because they can trap you into saying something that isn't true. For instance, I could say, "We never have any returns because we always meet all of our customers' needs."

First off, nobody is going to believe you, because they know it can't be true. It is much more accurate and effective to say, "We seldom have returns because we work very hard to meet our customers' needs."

One of my favorite selling words is "virtually." You can put it in front of a definitive such as, "We can meet virtually all of your needs." Bless your little heart.

"Say what you think with confidence when your words come from your heart. Embrace your mistakes for the lessons they teach. Treat burdens like small hills you will climb beyond. Laugh with those who laugh with you. Put forth your best and be proud you did. Do these things and peace will find you."
Liane Holliday Willey

Love What You Do

I have been blessed to work in sales for most of my career and have met a lot of wonderful people along the way. One friend comes to mind, Bill Maricic.

When things were stressful at the office, Bill used to call me out of the blue and say, "Hey, we could be outside digging ditches!" Other times he would call just to say, "Whatever doesn't kill you makes you stronger!"

I love people who are eternally optimistic and try to see the bright side of every situation. This is how I try to live my life as well. When you are working in sales, stay away from negative people. They have a problem for every solution. It is really important to foster a positive attitude when you are selling.

Over the years, I have had to disassociate myself from people who were just dragging me down. They seemed to sap my energy and give me a bad attitude. Nowadays, I am usually a very happy, positive person! If you have people in your life who are continually sapping your happiness and dragging you down, I strongly suggest you find a way to avoid them while at work if not altogether.

One of my peers, Lisa Burney, used to call me when she got frustrated with work. I always gave her the same advice—and it worked. I would say, "Lisa, go to the mall right now and buy a new pair of shoes." She always called me back in a much better mood and proceeded to tell me about her great new shoes. Then she would go make some sales.

Whenever I would make a big sale, I used to crank up James Brown's song, "I Feel Good!"

I also like balancing my sales days with happy calls. These are calls to existing customers whom I really enjoy spending time with. They help me recharge and go face the day calling on prospective customers.

What better profession could we be in than sales? I LOVE BEING IN SALES—most of the time. We get to talk with all kinds of people, laugh, smile, and have a good day! Or as my good friend and spiritual mentor Duke Heller likes to say, "Make it a good day!"

Love what you do and you will be successful!

"The only way to do great work is to love what you do."

Steve Jobs

Why Use a CRM?

Most companies nowadays require you to use a CRM (customer relationship management) database. Wikipedia defines a sales force automation CRM as follows:

"Sales force management systems are information systems used in CRM marketing and management that help automate some sales and sales force management functions. They are often combined with a marketing information system, in which case they are often called customer relationship management (CRM) systems."

In my experience, most salespeople would rather not spend their valuable time documenting each and every interaction with a customer or prospective customer.
You likely fall into this category, and that's OK.

So why does the company force you into the drudgery of painstakingly entering this information into the CRM? They do this for a variety of reasons.

For instance, the company's sales and marketing management personnel will have up to date information for their marketing efforts and can document the sales processes to help keep the upper-management number crunchers off their backs.

Plus, in your case, you probably won't personally work with those accounts forever. The CRM gives great information to whoever will work with those accounts in the future.

What is it that most salespeople really want from their companies that will help them make more sales? If you answered "good leads," you would be correct.

The cumulative information contained within the CRM gives the company a plethora of information to help you make more sales. For starters, it helps the powers that be know what products or services to put on sale and when to do it.

When new products come out, the company often has great success launching them by targeting the specific customers and prospective customers who are most likely to purchase. This of course means more sales, bonuses, and commissions for you!

Whether you are the only salesperson in your company or one of many, I highly recommend logging your customer and prospective customer interactions into a CRM. Used correctly, a CRM can be an excellent personal assistant.

CRMs can remind you when to follow up with someone, and they never forget! CRMs can help you forecast your upcoming sales by putting them into a model (sometimes referred to as a funnel) based on the likelihood and date of potentially closing the sale.

Use your CRM to make more sales and more money!

"A salesperson can be 100% process driven and be pretty successful. A salesperson who uses 100% people skills can be pretty successful. The ones who use 50/50 are pretty much unstoppable."

James B. Hasty

Using Multimedia

Multimedia can significantly enhance your sales presentations. If a picture is worth a thousand words, then, used correctly, a video can be worth a billion words. Since people make their buying decisions emotionally, a video can be a powerful tool to bring out emotions to help you sell. Just think back to the last time you walked out of a movie theater. There is a good chance you remember how you felt.

With the wide variety of small, inexpensive tablet computers available, there is really no excuse for not having your multimedia presentations with you on a sales call.

If your company doesn't provide you with a multimedia presentation, consider making a PowerPoint presentation yourself. If you can use Word, then PowerPoint will be fairly easy for you to learn. If you prefer Mac, consider using Keynote for Mac. There are a lot of free training videos and PDFs available on the Internet.

Your multimedia presentation can include text, graphics, photos, sound, and videos to help you make an effective sales presentation. When using videos, many people link to the video on their website or YouTube via the Internet. If you link to the Internet, it requires less space on your computer and usually runs very well . . . usually.

Sometimes the venue where you want to give your multimedia presentation is in an area of a building where you cannot access the Internet.

This is why I highly recommend making two versions of your presentations. Create one version to link to your videos on the Internet and one version to imbed the videos onto your computer. If your computer does not have much storage space, you can store these versions on an external flash drive.

Consider that a sales call could go so well that you would be asked to make a group presentation—right away. This is especially true in institutional and corporate settings. My wife bought me a very small, powerful multimedia projector that I now carry in my computer bag. I have used it on the fly for staff meetings and when another projector broke down.

Multimedia Presentation Guidelines:

- Keep videos less than a minute.
- Minimize text on the screen.
- Try to use graphics on every screen.

Now you are ready to make an eloquent multimedia presentation on the fly.

"It's been said that people pay attention to novelty, danger, and extreme emotion. So if you can present a new solution to someone's problem that replaces fear with excitement, you'll sell every time."

Fr. Joshua Wagner

Pick Up the Phone and Call

Nowadays with all of the different ways we can contact somebody, it seems like we use our telephones less and less for actually calling people. In fact, there is a significant trend toward not having a home phone at all, unless you need a fax line.

I have to admit that it is so convenient to just type out a random text, tweet, or email and then move on with our day. This, of course, can be an effective means of communication.

That said, there are potential downsides to these types of communication:

- Texting, tweeting, or emailing the wrong person or group of people

  o I have accidently "replied to all" when I was trying to say something regarding the whole group and intended it only for the sender. I don't know you well enough to give you the specific details, but suffice to say, it was quite embarrassing.

- o Since we are often picking a name from a list, it is way too easy to text, tweet, or email the wrong person with the right information.

- No voice inflection or tone to help communicate your true meaning

- In speaking, we can easily enhance our communication by changing how we say something. This is not so easy in written communication.

- Autocorrect

  - o When your computer or phone decides to randomly change what you write, it can be very interesting.

  - o My mom once wrote "Hip hip hurray!" in a response to some good news. Her autocorrect feature turned it into "Hippy parade!"

- Wrong attachments

- o You can't take back a wrong attachment.

- Easily overlooked

  - o There is nothing like working for an hour on the perfect email only to learn the person never received it, accidently deleted it, or lost it in the spam folder.

I share all of this to remind you that, in sales, your customer buys from you, the person. Pick up the phone and speak with your prospective client to be sure your message is clear and properly received.

The good news is that businesspeople are getting fewer phone calls these days because most communications are coming electronically.

The bad news is that you have to have the courage to pick up the phone and call them, even when you think they may not be happy to receive your call.

"In sales, it's not what you say; it's how they perceive what you say."

Jeffrey Gitomer

Ongoing Sales

Companies often focus on acquiring new business while taking their existing customers for granted. Cable companies and mobile phone providers are good examples. They often hold their existing customers to higher rates while courting new customers with lower rates.

As contracts expire, customers leave their current providers in droves and accept the offers at lower rates from competitive companies. Recently, I saved over $100 per month by changing my TV/Internet/phone provider.

When I called to cancel, they told me I should have called earlier and they would have lowered my monthly bill. Why didn't they call me?

I hope you will take care of your loyal existing customers so they won't be running out the back door while you are bringing new customers in the front door. If your attrition rate (business you are losing from existing customers) is 50% and you are trying to grow your whole business by 10% overall, you would need to bring in 60% new business to actually grow your territory by 10%.

Wouldn't it be better to court your existing customers and have to sell less new business? I recommend keeping your current customers happy and also getting some new business so you can have the best of both worlds.

Most customers just want to feel appreciated. If you have a business that requires residual ongoing orders from your customers, send them an email once a quarter thanking them for their business or even asking for their input about their experience with your company. It is best if you can call occasionally to let them know about any new products or company news, and also see how they are doing.

Another good way to keep your customers engaged is to have special sale prices "just for them" once in a while. You can also have monthly specials for them to look forward to.

Don't over-communicate, though. I bought some clothes recently at a fairly high-end clothing store. They asked for my email so they could send me specials, so I signed up.

Every day I got a new email with their deal of the day. It drove me nuts, so I unsubscribed and now I tend to avoid their store. I don't know what marketing geniuses came up with their daily email promotions idea, but they should be shot.

"Expect the best. Prepare for the worst. Capitalize on what comes."

Zig Ziglar

Office Software

Two popular office software programs you will likely need to master are Microsoft Word and Microsoft Excel.

The trend right now seems to be that companies' business software runs on Windows and the marketing department uses Mac for their graphics and videos.

I personally use both as well as Droid. It is important to stay up with technology in business to some degree, but don't feel like you always have to be on the leading edge (or "bleeding edge," as I like to call it).

One of the best office software applications I have ever used is spell check with autocorrect. One of the worst office applications I have ever used is spell check with autocorrect. I say this sort of tongue-in-cheek because, while spell check is wonderful, it has bitten me more than once.

One time we were sending a corporate communication to doctors that detailed how safe a certain piece of surgical equipment was during surgery. We stated that they would have an "atraumatic" surgery, meaning that the surgery would not be traumatic.

Spell check with the autocorrect feature changed the sentence to say "a traumatic" surgery, meaning that the surgery would be traumatic! Good thing we caught that one before it went out. Be sure to double check.

For some reason, my fingers have trouble typing the word "from" and it comes out as "form." Unfortunately, spell check lets it through because "form" is also a word. I hope that didn't happen when I typed the draft for this book! If so, blame my editors.

The lesson here is not to entirely trust Microsoft Word to keep you out of trouble when you are typing a business document.

Have someone else read any of your important documents before you send them. Trust me; you won't see some mistakes because you are too close to them. Reading your document out loud also works well when proofreading.

There are few things in your career that will tick you off more than having hours of hard work simply vanish. I still cringe when I think about a multi-page departmental budget spreadsheet I was finally finishing when it just disappeared — forever!

Nowadays I save most documents on the cloud so I can access them if my computer crashes. I recommend that you save and save often!

"Success is going from failure to failure without loss of enthusiasm."
Winston Churchill

Think for Them

When you are prospecting for new customers or trying to get more business from your existing customers — think for them. You are uniquely positioned to know more about your market, trends, upcoming events, and product enhancements than your customers.

I learned this when I used to sell dental implants to surgical dentists. They are highly educated medical professionals and I was just a new sales representative fresh out of training. To be honest, I was pretty intimidated. What could I possibly show them that they didn't already know?

Well, as it turns out, quite a bit. You see, they may know everything about their surgeries, but they didn't know nearly as much about dental implants as I did. I was able to show them the intricacies and nuances that were unique to my products, and so I often converted them to buy from my company.

It may surprise you to know that doctors, dentists, veterinarians, many PhDs, and the like get little to zero business training in school. That's right—you likely have more business training than they do!

This is a fantastic opportunity to become a resource to help these doctors grow their practices and businesses. I soon found myself being asked to lecture at their study clubs, residency programs, dental society meetings, trade shows and CE courses. This resulted in my sales skyrocketing.

You don't have to know everything about everything. You just need to know one thing better than your potential customers do: your product.

Then you can become a resource for them by thinking for them. You can anticipate their needs and keep them abreast of industry news and events. Once they know, like, and trust you, they will tend to depend on you and, of course, purchase from you.

Consider starting a blog for your customers or at least a page on LinkedIn or Facebook where you can personally send updates about your industry. Try to anticipate what they might be interested in and post it. Industry articles and upcoming industry events are usually well received.

Ask them to post things as well. Next thing you know, you become the go-to person, all because you think for them.

Start thinking of what you could share with your customers and prospects right now that would make you a resource for them.

"It's not about money or connections. It's the willingness to outwork and outlearn everyone."

Mark Cuban

Be Ready for Anything

When you are calling on customers and prospective customers, you are the face of your company to your prospect or customer. In essence, you are the company.

Customers will occasionally want you to take products they are returning to your company so they can save money on shipping. They would rather you spend your money to return their products. Sometimes I want to say, "Did I drive up in a big brown truck and drop this off here?" I guess you can't really blame them for trying to pass the buck.

If at all possible, very tactfully avoid taking any return products for your company. There are some significant downsides that could arise as a result of you taking responsibility for your customer's property:

• You could misplace it, forget to send it in, or send it in late.
• It could get lost or stolen in shipping.

• The company could mess it up on their end because it didn't come in through usual channels.

• Customers may say they gave you more than they actually did. Memories are short.

A quote from Oscar Wilde comes to mind here: "No good deed goes unpunished."

Another way to be ready for anything. When making sales calls, you often need a variety of company literature. If you see several clients and prospects during the day, it can be easy to run out, especially if all you have is what you put in your bag that morning.

Other salespeople have literature all over their back seat or trunk. I suggest using a plastic milk crate from the office supply store that comes with hanging folders to store your literature. You will have plenty for your day, and it is easy to inventory and restock—plus you can easily remove it from your vehicle.

If you have a meeting scheduled with an important prospective client, you can make a good impression by personalizing a folder and putting your company information in the folder. A nice-looking computer-generated label can go a long way toward separating you from your competitors.

Also, stash some extra business cards and pens in your car in case you run out or happen to forget them one day. You might want to keep some breath strips handy for those "coffee breath" and "lunch breath" days. Be ready for anything!

"Make your head save your heels."
Lawrence G. Hasty

Plan in Advance for Events

Trade shows, seminars, courses, and events are great opportunities for you to represent your company. They are often wonderful selling opportunities, because your prospective customers are away from their usual daily distractions and are often looking to spend some money while there.

Most of the salespeople who work these events will miss out on key selling opportunities. They tend to look at these events as social opportunities to hang out with other reps and party. Remember that you are there for one reason only, and that is to sell.

If you work an event properly — and I am a stickler about this — you will likely do very well. You may be surprised to find that working an event properly starts long before the actual event.

First off, somebody needs to register your company for the event. This often entails picking an exhibit location and maybe even providing a speaker for the event. It is important to sign up as early as you can to be sure that you get a good spot and also so you can interact with the people planning the event.

It is nice to have a positive relationship with the event planners.

Event planners often provide you with a list of speakers and attendees. This is good information to have before an event. See if any of the speakers are planning to promote your products.

Contact them and the other speakers to let them know you will be there and that you can provide product photos and marketing materials for them as needed. You might influence the core presentations at the meeting and blindside your competitors, who will never know what hit them.

Now you can start contacting the attendees in your territory to let them know you will be attending their meeting. Try to get to know them as best you can before the event so they are comfortable coming by your exhibit and spending time with you.

Also, make sure to provide the attendee list to any of your fellow company reps who will have attendees coming from their territories.

When the meeting starts, you will have a big advantage. In the off hours, try to hang out where the attendees are hanging out. You will get many chances to present your product while your peers are out partying.

"My Saturday was going pretty well until I realized it was Sunday."
Unknown

Remind Your Manners

When my daughter Shayna was little, she used to come up with some adorable statements. One of them was her version of "mind your manners." She would emphatically say, "Remind your manners!"

These days, Shayna Hasty is an outstanding salesperson in her own right. She will probably kill me for putting this in my book.

When working events, it is critically important to "remind your manners." You must be professional, polite, friendly, and available for your prospective customers.

I have walked through large exhibition halls in search of viable sales candidates for positions I had available at the time and found nobody I would hire. It is not that my standards are ridiculously high either.

Sadly, it is because theirs are too low.
Some reasons I wouldn't hire specific people working trade show exhibits: they

were wearing disheveled clothes, playing or texting on their phones, sitting down reading a paper, flirting with someone at another exhibit, all talking to each other, or munching down a meal at the booth.

Whenever I worked a trade show exhibit, and I have worked hundreds, I would act as though my exhibit were inside a Neiman Marcus store. The brochures and sample products would be neatly organized with no food or drink on the display, and I continuously scanned the participants so I could engage anyone who seemed like he might be interested in our products or services.

Here are some unwritten rules of trade show etiquette:

• Eat before you arrive.
• Set up early and be ready before the doors open.
• Stay until the last participant leaves the floor.
• Never engage a prospective customer at another company's booth.
• Don't cross your arms.

- Use a firm handshake when greeting someone.
- Do not interrupt a peer's sales presentation.
- Work your assigned spot and do not spend your sales time talking with your peers.
- Keep your booth neat.

At smaller events, the same rules generally apply along with some others:

- Speak quietly so as not to disturb the participants in the other room.
- When entering and leaving the room, do not let the door slam behind you.
- Do not sit with your peers at meals with participants, so you can divide and conquer.
- Never break down your exhibit before the meeting is over.
- And, of course, be sure to remind your manners!

"What you do speaks so loudly, I can't hear what you're saying."

James A. Burney

Understanding Your Bosses

When you work as a salesperson for a company, it is very helpful to have a boss who understands and supports what you do as well as what you need in order to be successful.

Some companies look at their salespeople as expendable personnel who take orders for the company's wonderful products that the customers are lucky to buy.

The best companies revere their salespeople as the critical faces of the company who bring in the revenue that pays everyone's salaries. Most companies fall somewhere in the middle.

Whenever I counsel a salesperson whose boss is inept, I tell him or her that bosses come and go and this one is likely on the way out.

Unfortunately, in large companies and institutions, managers can often survive indefinitely simply by saying "no" to anything new. This is especially the case with bosses who are close to retirement and do not want to rock the boat.

When you look at a company that you may consider working for, make sure you understand whoever is ultimately in charge of the company's sales organization.

If the boss came up through sales, you will likely be in good hands. More often than not, the boss came up through a different profession such as accounting, engineering, science, or marketing. I have worked under all of these.

If the boss is an accountant, he will want the numbers to work, so he tends to inadvertently raise the forecasts and tell the sales department what they "need" to sell.

If the boss is an engineer, she will tend to be a linear thinker and not very open to "out of the box" ideas that may be critical for growing sales.

Scientists tend to be narcissistic and live in their own worlds. Unfortunately, they can sometimes treat the sales people like a science project and are not very open to the human aspect or the actual things necessary to increase sales.

Marketers tend to view sales personnel as drones that deliver their well-thought-out marketing campaigns.

The good news is that you are the one bringing in the money for the company. Present your ideas in an unemotional, logical format, and eventually they will likely stick. Then, of course, your bosses may take credit for the ideas—but at least you will be increasing your sales!

"F.E.A.R. has two meanings—Forget Everything and Run, or Face Everything and Rise. The choice is yours."
Zig Ziglar

When It Hits the Fan

No matter how good you are, sooner or later, something is going to go terribly wrong with one of your products or accounts, or both. How you handle this will determine whether your customer chooses to remain your customer — or not.

You will need to garner every ounce of composure and integrity you can muster when a crises occurs. Remember, when the smoke clears, this too shall pass. As always, even when it is painful, honesty is the best policy. If you made a mistake, admit it. If something happens beyond your control, let your customer know as soon as possible.

Most people understand that mistakes happen, unfortunate circumstances arise, and acts of God such as severe weather are more powerful than your overnight shipping company. They can still get pretty upset, though! It is important to be calm and rational as well as to let your customer know that you and your company are diligently working toward an amicable solution to the situation.

In many cases, the same Chinese symbol used to write "crisis" is used to write "opportunity." There is generally an opportunity hidden inside every business crisis. It may be the opportunity to show others how you can step up and face the crisis head on. It may be the opportunity to bond more deeply with your customer.

I used to sell dental implants in Texas. One of my biggest customers was Dr. J. Hadley Hall. He had recently purchased a new line of dental implants from me that screwed into place and was unable to place one in the back of his patient's jaw because the implant carrier was way too long.

He called and very patiently said that the design engineers must work in a room with really tall ceilings, but that their implant carriers didn't work in his patient's small mouth.

This was a crisis for me! If he had returned his order, it would have reversed a big bonus check. Fortunately, because of our strong business relationship, he trusted me and accepted the opportunity to work out a compromise until the company came out with shorter carriers. We are close friends to this day, and he even contributed to this book!

No matter how bad it seems at the time, just be forthright, patient and find a solution.

"Something very beautiful happens to people when their world has fallen apart: a humility, a nobility, a higher intelligence emerges at just the point when your knees hit the floor."
Marianne Williamson

What's In It for Me?

A great way to approach anyone you meet is to pretend he or she is carrying a sign that says, "What's in it for me?" After all, we have to remember that we are dealing with individual, unique, emotional human beings.

Most often, people just need to be appreciated for who they are and what they do. Simply acknowledging that they are important goes a long way toward helping them decide to help you.

A sincere compliment can go a long way as well.

For instance, when you approach a receptionist, look at what she has chosen to display in her office. Notice her jewelry and work area. Surely you can find something to genuinely compliment her about, even if it is, "Nice chair!"

Once you have comfortably engaged this person in a conversation, she is much more likely to help you reach your prospective customer.

When you get to your prospective customer, pretend that he or she is carrying a "What's in it for me?" sign. As you begin your conversation, remember that this person is a unique, emotional human being who may well purchase from you — if he or she likes you.

Don't rush into your sales presentation. Look around the office at what the person has displayed. See if you can find common ground like sports, family, etc. If you can have a friendly interaction regarding a common interest, he or she will be much more likely to want to hear your sales presentation.

What are this person's career aspirations and personal business goals? Tailor your sales presentation to specific aspects of your product or service that you think may be personally of interest to your prospective customer.

We tend to assume business executives have everything well covered. Did you know that many surveys indicate that at least half of all executives feel they are in over their heads?

This is good information to know when speaking with business executives. Although I don't recommend sharing this information with your prospective business executive customer, it would be prudent to show how working with you could help this person achieve his or her goals.

Small business owners often feel overwhelmed as well. They definitely carry an imaginary, "What's in it for me?" sign. Become a resource to them, and they will become loyal customers.

"Things may come to those who wait, but only the things left by those who hustle."
Abraham Lincoln

Don't Bring Your Baggage

In sales conversations with customers and prospective customers, it is vitally important to remember that, in most cases, these are not your friends. The reality is that whenever you leave your company, you will probably never talk to them again. I know this may sound harsh, however it is often true.

The fact that this person is friendly and personable with you does not mean you are in his or her inner circle. The reason customers interact with you is because they have a relationship with you and your company that benefits them at the time.

These are not the people to vent your problems to. It is not appropriate to bring your personal or company baggage to your customers. Nobody except your closest friends and family cares to hear about your problems.

Think of it this way: Customers buy because they like and trust you. When you enthusiastically help them with their buying decisions, it makes them feel good. Then they want to continue buying from you in the future.

If for some reason you are disgruntled with your boss or your company, you need to keep it to yourself. If you go around complaining to people in your industry, you are going to start rumors that will ultimately affect your credibility as well as that of your company.

Remember, customers want to buy from people and companies they feel good about.

If you are having personal problems, you need to address them away from your work environment. Your job is to perform a necessary function for your employer to the best of your ability.

Your professional image is critical in your sales career. People in your industry do not need to know your personal situation, nor is it any of their business.

Unfortunately, many will kick you when you're down. Remember that there are plenty of people who would love to have your job.

A great way to use your emotions is to turn them into fuel that motivates you to do well in your business. Success is the best revenge! This applies to your physical wellbeing too. Nothing inspires a good workout at the gym more than being pissed off at somebody.

Once you've had success at work and a vigorous workout, you can come home and meditate, relax, and enjoy life.

"I've missed more than 9,000 shots in my career. I've lost more than 300 games. Twenty-five times I've been trusted to take the game-winning shot and missed. I've failed over and over again in my life and that is why I succeed."
Michael Jordan

Following Company Policies

Have you ever noticed that good salespeople are not very good at following the rules? This is actually one of the reasons they are successful.

If you really break it down and think about it, your prospective customers already have company policies in place for them to buy from their current suppliers.

A good salesperson has to convince these prospective customers not only to break their rules, but also to change these rules to buy from the salesperson's company.

Your company likely has many rules and regulations. Just like in government, rules and laws are often written because somebody did something that caused a problem for the governing entity.

Sometimes, of course, they are written to save the company money.

When I was an outside salesperson in Texas with a young family, I wanted to be home most nights if I could. Sometimes I would leave home at 5:00 AM and drive 200 miles to make an 8:30 AM appointment. Then I would make some cold calls, have a $10.00 lunch on my expense account, drive 200 miles back, and be home around 8:00 that night.

One day, the company bean counters decided that they would save the company some money and not allow salespeople to expense any meals unless they stayed overnight.

So I diligently followed their new company policies. I would leave the night before my 8:30 appointment and drive the 200 miles. Then I would stay in an $80.00 hotel room, have a $30.00 dinner, and then a $10.00 breakfast the next day before eating a $10.00 lunch on the way back.

Instead of spending $10.00 to be 200 miles away for a morning appointment, I would spend $130.00. After a while, the bean counters decided it was okay if I bought a $10.00 lunch on a 400-mile round trip.

To be fair, I have written numerous company policies and for good reasons.

The reality is that we need company policies in order to effectively manage a company and protect it from potential liabilities. In many cases, they can keep you out of serious trouble.

My point is that, just because company policies exist, it doesn't make them right. When I was the manager, I always told my salespeople never to let a company policy get in the way of common sense.

"Be so good they can't ignore you."
Steve Martin

Working With Your Peers

One of the great things about being in sales is that there are so many fun, smart, attractive peers you can associate with. When you are new to the company, most any of them will be happy to help you and answer any questions you may have.

In turn, you'll likely be happy to help the next new salesperson with any questions he or she may have. So what could possibly go wrong?

I wanted to put this section in the book to share some experiences and recommendations with you. Early in my sales career, I was flattered that the big company I was working for had chosen me to train incoming sales representatives.

I was very happy there, and I knew I could really help this new salesperson hit the ground with her feet running. After she had been my student for a couple of days, I could tell she was going to do OK, but she was still pretty green. In my opinion, she wasn't quite up to par with the salespeople in my class from the previous year. That said I was pretty sure I could coach her.

Then she made a comment about her salary, asking about when she would get a raise. As it turned out, the new class of sales representatives was being hired at several thousand dollars a year more than I was being paid!

I never shared that with her, but my morale suffered and I decided this wasn't where I wanted to continue my career. A word of advice: never share your salary information with your peers.

Peers who work together closely tend to get to know each other pretty well—too well. Be really, really careful about sharing your inner thoughts regarding your customers, other sales representatives or anyone else in the company.

A few innocent words over a drink can come back and hit you like a ton of bricks! Unfortunately, your peers don't always have your best interests at heart.

They are highly competitive and sometimes will use whatever means they feel are necessary to achieve their career goals, which may include throwing you under a bus.

A word about dating your peer salespeople — don't! The saying, "Don't get your meat where you get your bread and butter" is popular for good reason.

"People will always let you down. I will let you down. Jesus will never let you down."

Melvin Hinz

BEFORE YOUR SALES CALL

The Internet Changed Everything

Nowadays, before you can sit down with your customers, there is a pretty good chance that they have already looked up your company and its products on the Internet. This means they have likely looked up some of your competitors and their products as well.

Not only that, but they have also probably read good and bad reviews about your company, your products and could have a good idea what your prices are as well. If you are selling a commodity item, your potential customer can likely get a better price online.

You may be thinking, "Damn that Internet!" but let's not become so disenchanted quite yet.

The Internet works both ways. You also have the ability to thoroughly research your prospective customers and their companies.

If you are calling on a public company, there is an incredible amount of information out there about their stock, the value of the company, and the perceived health of the company. You can find out information with regard to their credit worthiness as well as any news articles, past and present.

Companies of any size usually have websites that you can explore to learn a wealth of information about the companies, their products and their people. There are also sites that rate the companies based on their reviews.

You can read pertinent reviews about most any company. Usually you can even see whether the reviews are actually from verified customers. (This is good because sometimes competitors and disgruntled ex-employees anonymously attack a company or a manager within the company out of jealousy, insecurity or spite.)

Not to mention you can look up your prospective customer on Facebook to get a feel for his or her lifestyle and personality. Then you can look the person up on LinkedIn to get a glimpse of his or her professional life.

You can even subscribe to sites like Spokeo and see things like where they live, their family members, the value of the home they are living in, and any court records pertaining to them.

You can look up the company's address on the Internet and automatically calculate the distance and driving time from your location to the office. You can even pull up a photo of the building and find local parking.

Now you can be thinking, "I love that Internet!"

"You are free to choose, but you are not free from the consequence of your choice."

Universal Paradox

Researching Your Prospective Customer

The days of cold-calling effectively by just walking in and trying to sell to someone you know nothing about are all but over.

We all think we are pretty good at "winging it," and we are, but the real money comes from properly researching your prospective customers before you meet them. Remember, you only have one chance to make a first impression.

That said, how does a salesperson have the best chance to make a good and memorable first impression? I think you would agree that the more you know about people, their business, their market, the competition, and their likely needs—the better chance you have to make a great first impression!

The best type of cold call is when a colleague of theirs refers you to them. This, of course, makes a great case for asking for referrals after you close a sale or even after someone has opted not to purchase at the time. In fact, when you can, ask them to call the person they are referring you to and introduce you.

If you must cold-call someone, try to learn as much as you can ahead of time. It is better to make one well-informed, focused cold call than ten random cold calls. This is much harder if you are selling "B to C" (business to consumer) rather than "B to B" (business to business).

There are many good ways to get relevant information about a potential customer. Start with an Internet search of his or her name and you will often find some great information such as recent awards, news articles, and memberships.

Also look the person up on LinkedIn and Facebook and see what you can learn. You can usually, at the very least, see what he or she looks like.

A personal LinkedIn profile can reveal outstanding information about someone's business or professional background. Try to get them to "link" you to their LinkedIn profile. In your request, you can say a little about you and your company as well as why you are contacting them. When you meet them in person, it will now be a warm call!

For your "B to B" selling, look up their website, local yellow pages, etc., and see what you can find out. You can virtually eliminate a true cold call.

"Selling is not about a slick presentation; it is identifying a need, and the filling or satisfying that need."

Robert W. Regan

What to Bring

By now, you have researched your potential customer on the Internet and determined that this person may be a prospect. You have reviewed any relevant data about this prospect in your CRM (customer relationship management) software.

I highly recommend making and using a checklist of common items you may need for your sales presentations. If you have to travel there, make and use a checklist of the necessary clothes, accessories, and toiletries for a business trip. Do you need to bring your name badge?

Make sure your shoes are clean and/or shiny, clothes are pressed, hair is neat, fingernails are presentable, teeth are clean, and breath is fresh before you enter the prospect's place of business. Bad breath has killed many a sale!

If you have company literature and/or sample items, make sure they are readily accessible during your sales presentation. It goes without saying that your business cards and a pen must be accessible also.

One of the worst things you can do to blow the rhythm and momentum of your sales presentation is to fumble when you need to pull out a piece of literature, a sample item, your business card, a pen, or especially your order form.

I mention your order form because I have seen so many salespeople neglect to bring order forms, especially to trade shows! You only have one job to do, so do it very well.

The cardinal sin in a good sales presentation is to not have an important item with you and need to send it to the prospect later. Most of the time, you can kiss that sale goodbye.

The second worst sin is when you must go back to your car to get something. You will lose all the momentum you have achieved thus far and basically have to start over — if the prospect still has time.

I say the sins of a good sales presentation because there are innumerable sins that can make for a bad sales presentation.

One of the best things you can bring to a sales presentation is documentation that proves what you are telling your prospect.

This can come in many forms; some examples are research articles, customer testimonials, and white papers. Although people tend to make their buying decisions emotionally, they must rationalize or justify them with logic.

"Without data you are just another person with an opinion."
W. Edwards Deming

Getting There

If you are an outside salesperson, you need to travel to your prospective client's home, coffee shop, place of business, etc. Many of you need to travel long distances in cars, on trains, or in airplanes.

The common denominator is that you must arrive on time and be ready to sell. There is no excuse for being late or not having your sales aids ready to go.

I have missed significant selling opportunities because I couldn't get somewhere on time. Some of the reasons that come to mind were driving the wrong direction on the freeway, canceled flights, staying too long at a previous appointment, being stuck in traffic, getting lost, inclement weather, and forgetting to put a meeting on my calendar.

Regardless of the reason, there is no excuse for a professional salesperson to miss a scheduled appointment.

Once, I was scheduled to speak to a study club for an hour on a certain day at 7:00 pm. Then the organizer called and told me that the whole society would be meeting that day and instead wanted me to speak at 7:30.

I had to travel to get there, so I decided to come in the night before and make some cold calls in the area on the day of the meeting.

At about 7:20 in the morning, I received an urgent phone call wondering why I wasn't already at the society meeting.

It turns out that the society meeting was at 7:30 am! So I had the organizer stall the meeting until I arrived around 7:45 . . . for an all-day lecture!

Fortunately I had enough with me to stretch an hour-long meeting into an all-day meeting, but it was pretty hectic for a while.

Since then, I have become a big believer in checking and rechecking appointments as well as getting everything in writing when possible, especially when I am the speaker.

Here are some tips for being on time:

• Drive by earlier to see exactly where you will be meeting and how to get there.
• Never take the last flight to a city, because if it cancels you are stuck.
• Fill your tank the night before.
• Plan ahead for construction zones and traffic.
• Call ahead to confirm your appointment.

If you are still running late, call and let them know.

"Ninety-nine percent of the failures come from people who have the habit of making excuses."
George Washington Carver

You Only Get One Chance to Make a First Impression

Chances are several other salespeople, including your competitors, have already met with the person you want to meet with today. Indeed, if this prospective buyer is on your radar, he or she is likely accustomed to meeting with salespeople and will decide right away whether he or she likes you enough to purchase from you.

Most current research indicates that people gather a significant first impression of you within the first second. It seems that among the fastest triggers are your voice and your facial expressions.

A genuine smile, friendly greeting, and firmly confident handshake can go a long way toward helping you make a positive first impression.

In sales, it is imperative that you do not meet with someone until you are feeling cheerful, confident and ready to sell. I have been known to drive around the block listening to upbeat music or even take a walk until I could become genuinely cheerful and confident enough to effectively sell.

How do you look? A lot of your confidence in how you carry yourself will come from knowing that you look your best. It may be somewhat acceptable to have wrinkled clothes, scuffed shoes, and messy hair if you work at a retail store or a fast food restaurant; however, it is definitely not acceptable for a professional salesperson to have a disheveled appearance.

How do you smell? Smell is a powerful sense that significantly contributes to making a good (or bad) first impression. Did you shower and use enough deodorant? Are you wearing cheap, overbearing cologne or even too much good cologne? If you are a smoker, be especially a cognoscente regarding how your clothes smell.

How about your breath? Bad breath is one of the biggest instant turn-offs anyone can have. Even coffee breath can damage someone's impression of you. Make sure you brush your teeth or at least take a breath mint before visiting your prospective customer. My wife got me started on breath strips, which are another quick and effective way to ensure your breath smells good.

What does your business bag look like? Does your bag represent your professional business demeanor, or is it simply a way to carry your materials? Are your materials and business cards readily available? Do you have everything you might need?

OK, let's go sell!

"Please be polite. Nothing in life should erode the habit of saying thank you to people or praising them."

Richard Branson

Rehearse Your Elevator Pitch

One of the most important things a salesperson needs to master is his or her elevator pitch. The term "elevator pitch" comes from the idea that you might suddenly end up in an elevator with your biggest prospective customer and have a matter of seconds to say something compelling and memorable.

This has actually happened to me, and it wasn't pretty. I choked and completely blew my unexpected opportunity.

We try to regurgitate whatever company line the marketing department wants us to repeat. These company mantras are well thought out by well-meaning marketing people in their offices.

The problem is that they are not (nor have most of them ever been) salespeople speaking to prospective customers in the heat of battle. These company mantras usually don't feel natural when you are actually saying them to someone. I suggest tweaking them slightly while keeping the same message the marketing department wants to get across.

We salespeople tend to take for granted that we can wing our 15-, 30-, and 60-second sales presentations and be fine. I am going to challenge you on this one. In my experience, 99% of salespeople suck at their elevator pitches.

Here is my challenge. On your smart phone, have someone record a video of you giving your elevator pitch. Then watch it by yourself, carefully and objectively. You are probably not going to be too happy with what you see, and that is OK.

I noticed that I tended to weave back and forth when I talked. I said "um" too much, and my delivery could have been much more eloquent.

We only get one chance to make a first impression, so why not master our elevator pitches and practice them often?

The other day, I attended the practice rounds at a major golf tournament. Even Tiger Woods, arguably the greatest golfer of our time, practices his swing.

If professional athletes have to practice, then I encourage professional salespeople to practice as well. One thing both have in common is that they make their money based on how well they can deliver under pressure at any given time.

Try listening to your elevator pitch with new ears, the ears of a potential customer. What does he or she really need to hear as the first impression of you and your company?

"Success comes through knowing and believing in you. Strengthen yourself in all you do; the rest will follow."

Steven Hanson

Walking In

Have your business cards, pen, and sales aids readily accessible. Make sure you look and feel professional and are ready to meet your prospective customer with a friendly greeting, a firmly confident handshake, and a genuine smile!

If you have an appointment, make sure you know exactly where you are going and how long it will take to get there at that time of day. Allow an appropriate amount of time for traffic as well as any potential inclement weather.

I once asked a judge if he allowed people to reschedule their court cases because of bad weather. He said if he could make it on time, he did not tolerate anyone else being late or not showing up. Neither will your prospective customers!

Also, make sure you have plenty of fuel and will not need to stop for gas. Plan to arrive at least ten minutes early. There is no excuse for being late.

Did you do your homework on your prospective customer before you came? There is really no reason for not learning as much as you can about your prospects and their businesses ahead of time. Even if you are making a cold call, you can use your smart phone to access the prospect's website before walking in.

Often there is information on the Internet that will help you find common ground with your prospect before your meeting. For instance, he or she may be featured in an article, on a board of directors for an organization, or a fan of a certain sports team. Most people have Facebook and/or LinkedIn accounts where you can see a wealth of this type of information.

Businesses often have websites that give you information about their products or services, management, philosophies, staff, etc. If they are publicly traded, you can easily look up their stock performance as well as a plethora of other information about the business.

Now, armed with this new information, you can be ready to discuss any number of topics that will help you find common ground with your prospective customer.

Also, as you walk in, take a look at whatever your prospect is displaying and be sure to compliment him or her on something. People tend to buy from salespeople they like, so do everything in your power to be likeable!

"Opportunity is missed by most people because it is dressed in overalls and looks like work."

Thomas Edison

Know Your Competition

I feel strongly that you must believe in your product or services, your company, and yourself so you can sell with confidence and integrity. This is true even if you don't have competitors approaching your customers and prospective customers, because it is only a matter of time before you do.

I have sold the premier product, cheapest product, clone product, commodity product, etc. Each segment of the market has its benefits as well as its drawbacks. To completely understand your products and services, you need to know where they fall within your given market as compared to the competitors, and what they are likely saying.

Sometimes you provide the exact same product or service, so you really have to separate yourself and your company from the other guys. How then can you differentiate yourself and your company from the competition?

You must become a resource to your customer. You are the one variable that will likely make the difference as to which company the customer chooses to purchase from. Your company may be the "great and powerful Oz," but you are the person behind the curtain.

Ultimately it is how you present to the customer that will make or break the sale. When people like what they purchased, they say that they "bought" it. When they don't like what they purchased, they say that the salesperson "sold" it to them. You want to sell it so well that, in the customer's mind, he or she bought it.

Typical Competition Differentiators:

• **Premier Product** – We are a market leader, dependable, will be here for you (yadda, yadda, yadda).

• **Cheapest Product** – We have the same thing for less. They are trying to make you pay for their research and development. They are ripping you off.

- **Clone Product** – Why pay so much for the same thing? Ours is interchangeable with theirs.

- **Commodity Product** – Trust me; we will supply it for you at a good price. I hear bad things about the other guys. We offer value-added services.

I was selling the clone product and the market leader decided to give away its products to our customers so that our customers wouldn't need to buy from us.

So we went to their customers and asked if they got their free products. We told them that the market leader was giving away products to their competition. The free product campaign abruptly ended.

"Be yourself. Take what you have studied, learned, and experienced and share your passion for your product, service, or mission with others. Be genuine. Be thoughtful. And follow up!!!"
Mary Beth Heffernan

Motivating Yourself

Making a living in sales takes a lot of self-motivation. Nobody is going to go out and sell your products for you. So what gets a good salesperson out of bed every morning?

For starters, you need to ask yourself why you have a job in sales in the first place. For me, it is because I like:

- Being my own boss
- That I am skilled at selling
- Flexible hours
- Travel
- Eating at nice restaurants
- The amount of money I can make
- Living the lifestyle the money affords me
- Helping people become customers so they can enjoy the benefits of my products and services
- Overcoming challenges
- Working with my friends in the industry
- Winning the sale

- Not working in a boring job
- Working with my brain and not my back

These are some of the same reasons you are in sales. Consider making a list for yourself to look at whenever you are feeling down or depressed. Sales is a great career!

That said, we all face more than our share of rejection. As a salesperson, you need to stay upbeat and enthusiastic so you can carry an aura that attracts people to you. Avoid negative people like the plague. The person who says it cannot be done should not interrupt the person who is doing it.

Most great salespeople get up early to handle their email, reporting, CRM, etc., and they are out the door before an average salesperson gets out of bed.

Top salespeople usually make time to work out, run, or swim most every day so they will have the energy and mental focus to be motivated and at their best. They also know that top salespeople at their competitors are doing the same thing.

Even the best of us get depressed and have to shake it off. Nobody wants to buy from a sourpuss.

Here are some anonymous words of wisdom from a motivational plaque that I like:

"When you start doubting — you start doubting yourself, remember how far you have come. Remember everything you have faced, all the battles you have won, and all the fears you have overcome. Then raise your head and forge on ahead knowing that you got this!"

So get back in your car, crank the music, smile in the mirror and kick some sales butt!

"While seldom instinctively easy, good salesmanship can become a learned habit. The payout for mastering a genuine desire to inform and educate while clearly communicating the need to purchase your product can be challenging but extremely rewarding."

Janet Fogt Casper

Reaching "C"-Level Executives

"C"-level selling to major corporations may be the crème de la crème of all selling opportunities. After all, these are the people who actually run the major corporations. These are the big decision makers, the CEOs, CFOs, CIOs, COOs, and the like.

Most of the time, in order to get the attention of the "C"-level officers in a company, you need to be selling something either very expensive or of strategic value to the company.

Perhaps you sell enterprise solutions, real estate, or major capital equipment. The process is still the same.

First you have to get onto their radar. Unless they are calling you because of an advertisement they read or a buddy referred them, you are going to have your work cut out for you for a while.

There are a number of potentially effective ways you may be able to make contact with your "C"-level prospects. You can:

Work your way up through middle-management personnel.

- Find the department managers of the department(s) that will utilize your products and try to arrange a meeting with them.
  - o Get them to want your products or services and ask their bosses to look at them.

Contact them on LinkedIn.

- There is a good chance they are on LinkedIn.
  - You can try to get them to "link" you to their LinkedIn profile.
  - You can also try sending an InMail.

Go directly through their secretaries.

- I like this approach because it is personal and the secretary has direct access to the boss.

o If you can win the secretary over, you have a great chance of meeting with your "C"-level prospect.

Send an email through the website.

- This works great for customer complaints. However, it is usually less effective in getting through to the "C"-level prospect, because it will be filtered out by lower-level employees.

Call on the phone.

- You can likely get a message to your "C"-level prospect if you call after hours and use the company name directory.
- If you call during business hours, you will probably get the secretary.

Mail personalized correspondence.

- This can actually get through, at least to the secretary.

- I prefer to send correspondence in a 9 x 12 flat envelope.
- Send correspondence via overnight delivery to make the biggest impact.

"Success is a mindset. Set your mind to SUCCEED!"

Laura Hasty-Worley

SELLING

Hasty Sales Presentation

Warm Up

A brief interaction talking about non-business — family, sports, etc.

- Try to talk about whatever is displayed in the office so you can find common ground and be likeable.

Segue

Skillfully change the subject to your sales presentation.

- "Speaking of touchdowns, I heard that your company had a great quarter of its own last quarter. Let's see if I can help you keep that going . . ."

Q&A (*Loading Your Gun*)

Ask discovery questions to learn more about issues that you and your company may be able to address. Reinforce the pain for an emotional component.

Let's say you are selling a cloud-based IT service:

"Do you mind if I ask you a few quick questions?"

- Thank you.

"Are your servers located in the building?"

- Alright.

"Has the system ever crashed?"

- It has?
- "Ouch!"

"How long was it down?"

- "Oh my, that couldn't have been good!"

"Did you lose any information?"

- "Oh no!"

Then move on to your next topic and repeat the process.

Write down information in areas where you might be able to offer some possible solutions. (*Bullets*)

- "What if I could show you a way to keep your system up 99.9% of the time?"
- "Would it be a benefit to you if your data could never be lost?"

Emotional Hook—Presentation specific to the needs expressed. (*Firing Your Gun*)

- (*First Shot*) "John, I have some good news for you! We can make it so you won't have to worry about your computer crashing anymore. It would be impossible for it to crash because we have triple backup systems."
- (*Second Shot*) "Remember how you felt when you lost all that data? We can make sure that never happens again. Your data will be securely stored on the cloud."
- (*Third Shot*) "We can do all that and more for less than $200 a month, which is only about $6.67 a day."

Summarizing

- "I think we have agreed that it is important to you to keep your company's computer systems operating and your data secure so you can keep your company running smoothly, right?

Soft Close (*Feeler*)

- "Does $6.67 a day seem reasonable to help keep your company running smoothly?"
- "Do you think you could make room for $6.67 in your budget?"

Close

- "Excellent! Shall we do it? OK, let's do it!"

"The great sales reps have confidence, humility, integrity, and true compassion."
Melissa Endo

Key Account Management

In sales and in business in general, 80% of your revenue typically comes from 20% of your accounts.

In some cases, certain key accounts can make up a huge part of your territory sales revenue. These are the 500-pound gorillas in your territory.

There are three problems with 500-pound gorillas:

1. **They know they are 500-pound gorillas.**

- They expect special treatment.
- They expect a ridiculously good deal.

2. **Your competitors also know they are 500-pound gorillas.**

- They are always trying to get the business.
- They will do most anything to get the business.

3.   **If he quits buying, it takes a whole lot of monkeys to make up his business.**

•   Your quota is based on his business.
•   Your commission and bonuses are based on his business.

Try to avoid letting your 500-pound gorilla know that he's your biggest customer. It is like the old joke, "What do you feed a 500-pound gorilla? Anything it wants!" So our job is cut out for us.

Ideally, we can nurture this gorilla and keep him as a customer. This requires a lot of finesse and patience.

The best scenario is that you can befriend this gorilla, his family, and his friends. In essence, become part of his inner circle. I have spent a lot of time, day and night, with 500-pound gorillas and their families.

You need to understand the basic premise of working with 500-pound gorillas. They are always hungry and they always want more.

So you need to dangle a big carrot. Something your company can help them acquire that might be difficult for them to acquire on their own.

It could be "making them famous" by having them become major speakers for your company or putting them in a commercial. A commercial could be a video on your website if your company isn't very big.

(For you ladies who are wondering why I say "him" instead of "him or her," it is because I am physically envisioning a big fat gorilla and well, I just didn't want to go there.)

To keep a 500-pound gorilla happy, you must find out his vision for the future and offer a reasonable promise of helping him get there. Then make sure to keep in close contact.

The other guys are just trying to sell their products to him.

"No matter how many mistakes you make or how slow your progress, you are still way ahead of everyone who isn't trying."

Tony Robbins

Loading Your Gun

When you get the precious opportunity to sit down and have a conversation with your prospective customer, be very patient and ask good questions.

After the initial formalities, when it is time to start selling, I like to ask the prospective customer what his or her vision is for the business. I also ask if it is OK if I take notes.

Then I very carefully listen while we interact and I take notes (or, as I like to call it, "load my gun"). Whenever he or she shares something that I, or my product, can help with, I write it down.

Usually there will be three to five things on my list that will help me sell to this person. Lawrence G. Hasty, my father and sales mentor, was a top salesperson for Xerox. His advice to me in selling was simply to "find a need and fill it."

Now that I have written down the needs I can fill, it is time to start guiding the conversation toward my solutions.

The best way to guide a sales conversation is by asking the right questions. Telling stories is also a great way to guide a sales conversation.

Make sure to bring your story back around to the sales conversation at hand. Otherwise, you will find yourself losing all your momentum and needing to start over.

This is particularly the case when you are selling in a team situation. One person can be really close to closing the sale and then the other person, feeling like he or she needs to interject something into the conversation, asks a totally irrelevant question or makes a statement completely out of context that crashes the partner's momentum on the spot. You can inadvertently do that to your coworkers, so be careful.

Assuming you are still on track with your sales conversation, it is time to move forward by asking the right questions from your notes. Ready to shoot your gun.

"If I understand your vision correctly, you would need 'X, Y, Z' to complete it, right? What if I showed you how we can provide 'X, Y, Z' for you? Would you be interested?"

Now you have a chance to shoot your gun with incredible accuracy, one bullet at a time, and help complete his or her vision!

"If you don't pay attention to detail, you won't get a second chance with the customer."

Dr. J. Hadley Hall

Feel Selling

When someone is shopping for a product or service, that person's decisions regarding what and when to buy are usually based on how he feels about it at the time.

Unfortunately, most salespeople tend to talk mostly about the features and advantages of their products and services.

Newer salespeople tend to "show up and throw up" instead of listening intently to the reason someone is considering a purchase.

Consider that the reason this person is looking to buy is that he will feel good once the purchase is made. Maybe something has been bugging him for a while and this purchase will make him feel better in the long run.

Our patio and siding were gradually getting dirty and moldy. After a while, I realized that this was beginning to really bother me to the point that I wasn't spending much time on the patio. I finally bought a pressure washer to clean everything up and I loved it! I enjoy spending time outside now. It makes me feel good.

No doubt it is important to communicate the features and advantages of your products and services to your prospective customer. These things help customers logically rationalize and justify their purchases — once they feel like buying. You feel me? (Sorry, I couldn't resist.)

Before I go further, I need to stress that it is important that you personally believe in your products and services. Feel selling works best when accentuated with enthusiastic sincerity.

When I am selling to someone, you will hear me use phrases like these:

- "You are going to love . . . !"
- "Imagine how you good are going to feel when . . . !"
- "Your boss is going to love you . . . !"

- "You are going be so happy . . . !"
- "Your wife is going be excited . . . !"

You can also turn a feel close around when necessary. In that case, you might hear me say something like this:

- "How are you going to feel if you miss out on this?"
- "You know you are going to feel like crap if you don't . . . !"
- "You are going to hate yourself for not . . . !"

It has long been said that people buy on emotion and justify their decisions with logic. Create feelings in them that they will remember.

"I have learned that people will forget what you said, people will forget what you did, but people will never forget how you made them feel."

Maya Angelou

Getting and Using Referrals

Leads are the lifeblood of most any sales department. The best kinds of leads are the friends, colleagues, and family members of your happy customers. This is true, of course, only if they have a potential need for your products and services.

Surprisingly, salespeople often do not ask for referrals after they close a sale.

Some "B to C" (Business to Consumer) companies teach their salespeople to try to get their new customers to fill out a long, obnoxious list of possible referrals. This is not what I am recommending.

Admittedly, it takes some courage to take an order from your new customer and immediately ask that person to help you sell to someone she knows.

This, however, is exactly what you need to do. Strike while the iron is hot and she is emotionally engaged in the purchase!

Later, you may not even be able to get easy access to your new customer.

I am not asking you to give her a long, pathetic speech about how you survive on referrals and it is how she can show you that you have done a good job (yadda, yadda, yadda).

I am encouraging you to ask a simple, non-abrasive question. After thanking your customer again for the order, ask: "While I am here, can you think of anyone else who might benefit from using my products?"

Notice I didn't use the word "purchase" or "buy." I used a soft approach so as not to scare the customer away from helping me. Who wouldn't want their peers to "benefit" from "using" something?

If there is time, ask your new customer if she would mind giving her peer a quick phone call to introduce you. If not, ask if you can tell her peer that your new customer asked you to call.

Be enthusiastic when you make the call, and tell him or her that you have a happy new customer who asked you to call. Then keep the momentum going by asking if you could drop by and show him or her this great product while you are in the area.

Once you give your presentation to the new person, ask: "While I am here, can you think of anyone else who might benefit from using my products?" and then repeat the process and so on.

"The only place where success comes before work is in the dictionary."
                              Donald Kendall

Farmers, Hunters and Apex Predators

One analogy with reference to salespeople is that there are farmers and there are hunters. I like to add a third character to this analogy — the apex predator.

Farmers plant their seeds with their prospective customers, water them, add a little sunshine, and wait around in the hopes that sales will come so they can harvest their sales when the time is right.

Hunters, on the other hand, are not comfortable sitting around and waiting, so they go out in search of sales to hunt down.

Apex predators are at the top of the food chain, they are highly intelligent and they leave nothing to chance.

Apex predators thoroughly research their environment and their prey in advance. They carefully prepare ahead of time and go after only the best prey. Apex predators patiently stalk their prey until they decide the time is right to close in.

1. **Researching**
    - You are an apex predator looking for your next meal. Apex predators don't wander around aimlessly; they focus.
    - They anticipate where their prey will be and study the environment.
    - Seldom do apex predators aimlessly dive into a group of prey hoping to catch one. Apex predators identify their best target; they focus on one animal to be their prey.

2. **Warming Up**
    - Apex predators let their prey get comfortable and relaxed; they do not rush in and spook their prey.

3. **Understanding Needs**
    - Apex predators seek to understand the needs of their prey.

4. **Anticipating Objections**

- They see there is safety for their prey in staying in a group and not venturing out alone.

5. **Overcoming Objections**
   - Apex predators skillfully follow their prey to the path of least resistance — the watering hole.

6. **Offering Evidence**
   - They look at indisputable evidence supporting their position:
     - The prey needs water to live and must eventually go to the watering hole.
     - The apex predator has been successful 82% of the time at the watering hole.

7. **Summarizing**
   - The apex predator reviews the agreed needs and how it can successfully address these needs.

8. **Closing**
   - Everything else seems to be in order, so it is time to close in for the kill.
   - Success!

9. **Following Up**
   - The apex predator can eat on the carcass several more times if it can keep the competitors away.

Welcome to the hunt, my friend!

"Get Some"

3rd Battalion, 5th Marines

Selling to Different Personalities

Oftentimes, you can make an educated guess about someone's personality by the profession he or she chose to pursue. What personality comes to mind when you think of a librarian?

Does a completely different personality come to mind when you think of a news anchor? It wouldn't make sense to treat both types of people the same when you are selling to them, would it?

How would you approach and sell to an extroverted people person? I suggest an enthusiastic handshake and maybe a couple taps on the shoulder.

These people are impulsive and will likely respond well to how your product or service will make them look good to their peers. They can enjoy a lengthy conversation and sales presentation. They often react well to flattery and recognition, especially in front of others.

Let's compare that to an extroverted person who is not a people person. These people often come across as aggressive or bullies.

I suggest approaching them with confidence while being direct and to the point. They respond well to a one-page executive summary and a very short, informative sales presentation.

Do not try to bluff these people. They tend to let you know where you stand with them, so trial close them often and go from there.

Then there is the introverted people person. These people tend to work well in a support function, such as the right hand to a manager or the spouse of a dynamic executive. They tend to avoid the limelight, but they respond well to flattery and appreciation.

This could easily be the receptionist you are about to meet. They will often engage in an open conversation and a lengthier sales presentation, especially with multimedia.

They will also need clear direction from you as to what you are specifically asking of them.

What about the introverted person who is not a people person? This is your scientist or accountant type who likes to dig into the details.

They will be skeptical and looking for you to prove your points. They do not usually respond well to lengthy sales presentations and their critiques can be brutal.

They will need research, peer reviews, etc., and will require more time to make a buying decision.

Understanding the differences in people's personalities can be a powerful tool to help you sell.

"When I was five years old my mother always told me that happiness was the key to life. When I went to school they

asked me what I wanted to be when I grew up. I wrote down 'happy.' They told me I didn't understand the assignment, and I told them they didn't understand life."

John Lennon

Selling Over the Telephone

Selling over the telephone is an important skill to master for any salesperson. Whether you are in customer service, inside sales, or outside sales, when you are selling over the phone, you are the voice of the company you represent. As such, you need to be professional, articulate, confident, well organized, and persistent.

These days, selling over the phone is becoming a bit of a lost art. So many salespeople have become dependent upon email that they spend less and less time actually talking to their customers and prospective customers.

Email is a wonderful way to communicate. However, it also has some downsides when compared to selling to someone over the phone:

- No way to ensure they actually read the email

- Risk of mistyping email addresses
- Risk of your email going into their spam folder
- Possibility of your email getting lost in the shuffle
- Easy to misinterpret meaning conveyed in your email (no voice inflection)
- No sense of urgency to read your email

On the phone, it is easy to engage someone, and you know that person is hearing your message in real time. You generally get a pretty good indication of where you stand when you are speaking with someone on the telephone.

Here are some things you can do to enhance your ability to sell over the telephone:

- Try to have a quiet environment.
  - o You want them focused on your voice, not the dog barking or the TV in the background.

- Use a mirror and smile when you dial or pick up a call.
  - o People can hear a smile in your voice.

- Wear your nice business clothes even though they can't see you.
  - o Subconsciously, you will be in business mode and more focused.
  - o You won't easily become distracted.

- Use a phone script.
  - o You will make sure to convey all of the necessary information.
  - o When saying the same thing over and over on multiple calls, you won't have to remember if you already told somebody something.

- Stand up when you need to finish the call and they want to keep talking.
  - o Your demeanor will change and they will sense it.

- o It lets your blood flow and increases your focus.

- Set a minimum daily number of outbound calls.
  - o It helps keep you working and on task.

"The man at the top of the mountain didn't fall there."

Vince Lombardi

Selling to Doctors

I have had the honor and privilege of selling surgical equipment to many types of doctors throughout the world—from dental offices to veterinary schools to the operating rooms at the prestigious Mayo Clinic.

Have you heard what the difference is between God and a doctor? God doesn't think He's a doctor!

Seriously, though, physicians are among the smartest and most gifted people in the world. They have to endure years of training, pass local boards, and keep their continuing education up to date so they can have you as a patient. Many of them literally save lives every day.

One of the drawbacks of selling to doctors is that they really don't need you. They are set in their ways and like to purchase what they need from their usual vendors. They usually have staff members do their purchasing.

If they work at a hospital, the hospital purchasing department decides which vendors to purchase from. If a doctor wants to add a new product, it can be an uphill battle. Many hospitals buy through GPOs (group purchasing organizations), so your best bet may be to meet with your local GPOs and promote your products through them.

It can be really difficult to get a doctor to take time to sit down with you to listen to your sales presentation unless he or she called you.

This is when I recommend getting to know the staff. They can make or break you in a doctor's office. If you can convince the staff that the doctor needs to meet with you, there is a pretty good chance the doctor will eventually take the time to do so.

Bring your short sales presentation because doctors think fast and typically do not want a bunch of fluff. Usually, you will have ten minutes or less to make your case.

Have peer-reviewed articles favoring your product if possible.

Also, bring any white papers or research. If the doctor buys in and likes you and your company, you have a fair chance of making a sale. Become a resource for them because they likely have little to no business training.

Another tip: I always like to be where the doctors are going to be, such as local study club meetings where they are out of their element and less distracted.

"God has created a seed within each individual. Securely plant the root of that seed with trust and integrity. Encourage and that seed will begin to develop character and a vision. Nurture with discipline. The seed will then grow into a person who will exceed ones expectations and become a leader who is able to cultivate the seeds of others."

Kent Leighty

Selling to Engineering Specifications

My first outside sales position was selling for a water well pump company. I had worked my way up from warehouseman to warranty repair manager to purchasing/inside sales to field sales representative. I was in my early 20s and feeling pretty good about myself.

The first time I had a chance to work with the government, I had to learn the process. The purchasing agent provided me with a "request for bid." I had to review the specifications to see if I had a product (in this case, a pump system) that fit within the engineer's specifications.

I went to the sealed bid opening. There I was with a few of my competitors who had obviously done this before. Each envelope was opened ceremoniously by the purchasing agent and eventually the bid was awarded. I got my butt kicked! Not so much on price but because my pumps didn't quite fall within the specifications.

A month or so later, I went through the same arduous process again with the same results. Albert Einstein's definition of insanity is, "Doing the same thing over and over again and expecting different results." That pretty much fit my reality at the time.

Being a quick learner, adaptable, and highly competitive, I had an epiphany. There had to be a government engineer working on the next project somewhere nearby right now.

What if I could sit down with that person and get him or her to write the specifications so that only my company's pumps would fit the specs?

I went back and looked at my failed bids with a new perspective. I found the name and address of the engineer who wrote the previous specifications. Then, with a box of donuts in hand, I drove over to see him one morning unannounced.

He was a great guy, and I sold him on the benefits of working with me personally.

You see, he was an expert at engineering, but I was an expert on water well systems.

After that day, I helped him design every new water well system request. Somehow they ended up requiring specifications that only my products could fulfill. I bid high and those other guys all had to buy from me if they wanted to bid those specs.

I never lost one of those bids again.

"The harder I work, the luckier I get."
Jan Holliday

Selling Capital Equipment

For the purposes of this book, we will define capital equipment as goods that cost more than $5,000 and have an expected usage lifespan of more than one year.

The first challenge in selling capital equipment is that it costs a lot of money. A purchasing agent cannot usually order capital equipment as easily as ordering lesser-priced items like office supplies.

In my experience, the person requesting the purchase of capital equipment usually has to submit a purchase requisition (also called a purchase request or request for purchase order) to the purchasing department.

First, the purchasing department must secure the appropriate funds from the budget. Then the department usually sends bid requests to potential vendors whom they feel may be able to supply the capital equipment. This is when your company has the chance to submit its bid (best price) to the purchasing department.

Writing the bid may not be as easy as it sounds on the surface. Your competitors are likely writing bids as well. If you get too greedy, you could easily lose the sale. If you scrape the bottom of the barrel to offer the lowest price, you may not make any money on the sale.

Does your equipment require disposable accessories in order to function? Should you bundle them into your bid and make it a larger order? Should you just bid the raw capital equipment and let them deal with the accessories later? Should you send multiple bids?

Don't sweat it. There is a time-honored method to help you decide what would be best for your prospective customer. Pick up the phone to call and ask the purchasing agent what he or she recommends. Most of the time, these people are happy to help you. It makes their job easier.

It is not uncommon for a department to have the authority to write their own purchase orders for items below the capital equipment threshold, say up to $2,000. One department at a hospital I worked with really wanted a bundled package I was selling that cost approximately $10,000. The purchasing department turned down the purchase request.

Here's how I was able to get the sale. We broke the bundle into five separate $2,000 invoices. They then wrote five $2,000 purchase orders, I got my $10,000 order, and everyone was happy.

"There's winning, and there's everything else."

Steve Yzerman

Selling Through Dealers

Dealers are a great opportunity to help you sell your goods and services. You have the chance to magnify your efforts times the number of sales representatives employed by your dealer.

The challenge when working through dealer organizations is that your product is only one of many in their salespeople's bags. Some dealer organizations literally have thousands of products in their catalogs.

Working with your dealer's salespeople is a lot like being a regional sales manager, except that you do not have any direct authority over the salespeople. It can be a bit like herding cats.

It can also be extremely rewarding. Remember that your customer is the dealer and the dealer's customer is the one who purchases your product from the dealer.

When your company is just beginning to work with a dealer or if the dealer is a new account for you, this is what I recommend to get you started:

- Get a list of all of the dealer's salespeople.
    - These are your customers and you will need to nurture them.

- Acquire a copy of the dealer's company organization chart.
    - Learn who is in charge and who their bosses are.

- Give a formal presentation at the next sales meeting.
    - This is easier and more effective than training numerous salespeople individually.

- Meet with the dealer's sales manager to design an effective working strategy.
    - Get his or her buy-in or you will have an uphill battle with the salespeople.

- Meet with the top salesperson and win him or her over with your skill and charm.
  - o The other salespeople will call this person to see if he or she buys in to you, your product, and your company.

- Set up a training conference call with the dealer's salespeople and their sales manager.
  - o Enthusiastically present your products and services.
  - o Make sure to emphasize the benefits for the dealer's customers.
  - o Ask the sales manager and the top salesperson to tell the group what they like about working with your company.
  - o Give everybody your contact information and ask them to call you any time with questions, even if it is on the weekend.
  - o Arrange ride-alongs with the top salespeople ASAP.

- They will help you influence the others.

Always be professional and never gossip about anyone with the dealer's salespeople.

"Work like there is someone working 24 hours a day to take it all away from you."
Mark Cuban

Meeting with "C"-Level Executives

Congratulations! You have the opportunity to sit down with a "C"-level corporate executive and give your sales presentation. Depending on what you are selling, be prepared for him or her to bring other management personnel to the meeting.

A good "C"-level executive will read you like yesterday's newspaper, so you really need to be on your game. You will probably not be asked to come back if any of the people in the meeting feel that they do not want to work with you or your company.

Notice that I used the word "feel" and not "think." You likely have a viable product or service they are interested in, so they already "think" they may want to purchase it.

Here is a checklist of things to think about that will make them feel you are worthy of their business:

- Be on time.
    - o Go to bed at a reasonable time and get a good night's sleep.

- Get up early and eat a nutritious breakfast with lots of protein.
    - o You can crash in your meeting if you only eat carbs for breakfast.
    - o Plan to be at least 20 minutes early in case of unforeseen weather, traffic jams, trains, or construction.

- Look, act, and smell professional.
    - o Wear a conservative suit, clean and pressed (dark suit preferred).
    - o Wear a conservative shirt or blouse, clean and pressed.
    - o Wear new shoes or shoes that look new.
    - o Wear conservative socks that match your suit.

- Do not wear cologne or perfume.
    - o If you must wear cologne or perfume, use it sparingly.

- Come with your teeth recently brushed and clean.
    - o Use breath freshener if you had coffee or tea.

- Properly greet everyone.
    - o This includes the secretary and receptionist.

- Shake hands, smile, and be confident and friendly.
    - o This is not the time to flirt.
    - o This is not the time to joke around.

- Exchange business cards.
    - o This is a formality. However, it will provide great information for following up.

- Have folders prepared with pertinent sales aids inside.

- o Ideally, personalize these folders for each attendee. Resist the temptation to stuff these folders with a plethora of marketing materials.

- Make your presentation succinct.
  - o Show enough to get their interest.
  - o Keep it short.
  - o Leave time for questions.

"For God did not give us a spirit of timidity, but a spirit of power, of love and of self-discipline."

2 Timothy 1:7

Selling to "C"-Level Executives

"C"-level executives at major corporations are among the smartest people you will ever meet. When you put your presentation together, ask yourself this question: "What is important to a 'C'-level executive?"

It is highly likely that you will be expected to have a multimedia presentation. This could be a PowerPoint on a slide screen in their boardroom or possibly even on your laptop or tablet computer.

Other managers will probably be asked to attend your presentation. Ultimately, you want these people to leave your meeting wanting to buy from you emotionally and equipped to justify their purchasing decision with logic.

Tell them what your presentation is going to say, make sure you say it in the presentation, and finish by reminding them about what you told them.

Suggestions for framing your presentation:
Introduction:

- When you start your presentation, give a little pertinent information about yourself and then ask each participant to do the same.
  - This will help you understand what you are up against.
  - People like to talk about themselves, so this exercise tends to make them feel good as well.

- Start with your company logo, name, and title, plus a photo of your company headquarters if possible.

- The second slide should be customized to your particular audience — perhaps their company logo that you acquired from the Internet, a title for your presentation, and the date.

- The meat of your presentation needs to be succinct and interesting.

- o Use minimal text to engage their left brains.
- o Show graphics and pictures to engage their right brains.
- o Avoid overusing animations and flashy transitions.
- o Use a short video, if possible, for some emotional impact.

- Speak in terms of "benefits" to their company.
  - o Bring the benefits back around to anything they told you is important to them.

- Then support them with emotional statements:
  - o "You will love our company because . . ."
  - o "You will be so happy you made the decision to work with me."

- Summarize the benefits.
  - o "John, you won't have to worry about missing the deadline."
  - o "Lisa, you will love the new look."

- Thank them. Then wrap the meeting up and ask how they would like you to follow up.

Be sure to send thank-you cards to each participant with something customized to the benefits they liked. Follow up!

"The Lord *is* my light and my salvation; whom shall I fear? The Lord is the strength of my life; of whom shall I be afraid."

Psalms 27:1

When and How to Follow Up

You have given your sales presentation and submitted your written proposal. Now you are waiting to hear whether or not your prospect is going to purchase from you.

If this is a big opportunity for you, the anxiety you feel is likely similar to when you first exchanged phone numbers with someone you really hoped to date and were waiting to speak with that person on the telephone.

So what should the next step with my prospective customer be? The next step varies from situation to situation. However, I will give you some things to think about.

It is always a good idea to send a thank-you card after your initial sales presentation. In these days of lightning-fast electronic communication, a simple, old-fashioned, hand-written thank-you card can go a long way.

You might even consider including an assumptive "feel close" like, "I know you are going to love our company!" You should send a thank-you card to everyone who attended the meeting as well as the secretary or whoever set the meeting up for you. Send these right away.

It is critically important to get the details correct in a thank-you card. If you spell the person's name incorrectly, you can blow the whole effort. If your grammar or spelling is poor, the person will lose some confidence in you. Also, try to write cleanly and neatly so he or she can easily read the card and it looks professional.

If you have a "champion" in the organization such as the secretary, consider touching base within the first few days, ideally after the thank-you cards have been received.

I like to say something like, "I don't want to be a pest. However, I wanted to thank you again for setting up the meeting and also touch base to see how things are looking since the meeting." This is non-confrontational and shows that you genuinely care.

You can also follow up with the decision maker. Most people send an email. However, a phone call is much more powerful.

The worst thing your prospect can do is not take your call. If he or she does take your call, be polite and direct. Find out if he or she has made a decision yet and also if there are any questions you can help answer. Good luck!

"If I had given up after being turned down by banks 242 times, there would be no Starbucks."

Howard Schultz

CLOSING

Bite-Sized Pieces

Sometimes when we want to buy something, we just aren't comfortable with the financial outlay at that time. Think about the last time you saw a luxury car commercial on television.

They get you thinking about how nice it would be to cruise around in this luxury car.

They don't say, "For only $60,000 plus tax, license, and delivery, this high end luxury automobile could be yours!" We would probably change the channel.

How do they move these $60,000 cars off their lots and into their customers' driveways? They break the purchase into bite-sized pieces. "Sir, you can lease this car for only $675 per month." Now it is a whole different conversation.

After all, $675 per month is really only $22.50 a day. In fact, if I back off on buying those fancy coffees in the mornings, it would practically be free. I'll take it!

I was selling surgical equipment at a seminar, and I really needed to close one more deal. A doctor had been hemming and hawing on a quote I gave him for $18,000.

I showed him how he could get it for around $300 a month for five years. He still wouldn't take the plunge and time was running out.

Then I showed him that $300 a month was really only $10 a day. He wanted it, but he was still holding out and the meeting was almost over.

Finally, I walked up next to him in the back of the lecture room and nudged his elbow with my elbow. I looked at him disappointedly and whispered, "You can't afford ten bucks a day?" We installed it in his office three days later.

These surgical devices utilized reusable cutting tips that sold for about $300.

Doctors always balked at the price, so I had to come up with a way to ease their pain.

I would say, "I know it seems expensive. However, when you consider that they can be used for 20 different surgeries, they really only cost $15 per surgery. That's not so bad, right?"

If they still balked, I would ask, "Doctor, how much do you charge for each of these surgeries?" I usually got the order.

You may not want to read a 20,020-word book, but you might read 385 words — 77 seconds at a time!

"Challenges are what make life interesting; overcoming them is what makes life meaningful."
Joshua J. Marine

Benefit Closing

In selling, we are often taught to present a feature of a product or service and then explain why it is an advantage to the customer.

A cable company salesperson might be selling to a prospective buyer who has satellite TV. The feature might be that the cable is hardwired to the television. An advantage is that cable is not affected by weather. Then the salesperson moves along.

Stop right there! It is very important to get the prospective buyer emotionally involved in this conversation, because ultimately buying is an emotional decision.

Ideally, the salesperson has already asked a number of leading questions to discover the satellite customer's pain, but that is another conversation.

Whenever you present a feature and an advantage, your customer is likely thinking, "So what?" You need to get into the habit of proactively adding a "so that . . ." to your feature and advantage. Let's revisit the sales presentation and add a "so that" benefit to get the buyer emotionally involved.

"The cable is hardwired to your television. This means it will not be affected by weather so your television won't cut off in the middle of your show and you will be able to watch severe weather updates to know if a tornado might be headed your way." Now we have her attention!

After I present a benefit, I like to clarify whether it is a factor in the person's mind. An easy way is to simply add, "Would that be important to you?" after your benefit statement.

In closing, I like to recap the benefits the customer said would be important to her. I would start like this, then add any benefits she liked: "I think we've agreed that you don't like it when your show cuts off in the middle of a storm and that you'd also like to be able to watch severe weather updates when necessary."

Then close with something like, "If I could provide you with a service that would virtually guarantee you could enjoy uninterrupted shows, severe weather updates, etc., would you be willing to switch?"

Also, consider using the benefit first in your presentation: "With cable, you won't have to worry about not being able to watch severe weather updates during a storm because the cable is hardwired to your television!"

"Create an environment with your customers such that you are just an order-taking friend and supporter, not a salesperson."

Bill Ryan

If You Were Me

I have been blessed with many great mentors in my sales career. One of them was my late Uncle Ron, Ronald James Hasty to be precise.

One day after being rejected by some prospective customers and feeling pretty down, I had lunch with my uncle and mentor to see if he could cheer me up.

Years before, I had come to him when bullies at school were teasing me by calling me "Kenny" like I was some little kid.

He had once had the same issue with bullies calling him "Ronny." I will share his advice, which I still use today. He said, "Oh that's easy. I just told them that only people who loved me could call me 'Ronny.' " Shortly after that, only people who loved me called me "Kenny."

Regarding being rejected in business, Uncle Ron told me about a situation he had encountered as a young salesperson in the food industry.

When you sell to a grocery store, just like in real estate, the amount of square footage and location are very important. In the grocery business, this is called "shelf space." If your products don't have much exposure because they are only allotted six inches of space on the bottom shelf, you are not going to sell much.

This wasn't usually an issue because my uncle represented a major company and their products were always featured prominently by grocery stores.

However, at one store, the manager had an issue with my uncle's company and wouldn't allow adequate shelf space or the proper location needed to prominently display the company's products.

Uncle Ron met with the manager in his office and tried to no avail to get better shelf space for his products.

After he had all but given up, he went back into the manager's office and asked the manager if he could ask a favor. When the manager said yes, my Uncle Ron simply asked one question: "If you were me, how would you sell to someone like you?"

The manager seemed to like being a mentor to my young uncle and proceeded to school him. My uncle became a willing student and eventually had the best shelf space in the store.

Successful people often like to be mentors. Don't be too shy about asking them for their help.

"Sales: quite possibly the noblest of business occupations; when the salesperson seeks a 'win-win' outcome with the customer."

Brad Hansen

Some Closing Techniques

When I was learning to fly an airplane, it amazed me how easy most of it was. Taking off is like entering a freeway. Flying is like driving a car that also goes up and down.

Landing a plane—now that can be very difficult. You have to do everything right or you are going to crash. My first landing was pretty rough.

My flight instructor said, "I hope you aren't going to call that a landing. At best, it was an arrival!"

My first close was probably "an arrival" as well. In closing, like landing, you have to do everything right or you are going to crash.

Closing should be the natural conclusion of a sales presentation. Before you close, you want to have engaged the prospective customer emotionally, presented your products or services eloquently, and made him or her realize the benefits of buying from you and your company.

Closing, like all of selling, comes down to your personal style. I know some salespeople who successfully use colorful closing techniques to disarm their prospective customers, such as:

"Doctor, get over yourself!" – *Beth Hanson*

"Bitch, you be crazy not to buy this." – *Ashley G. Alsip*

Most closing techniques are much more conventional. One of my favorite closes is the "alternate choice" close. This works well because it doesn't give your prospective customer a simple "yes" or "no" choice.

It encourages him or her to pick one of your options. "Would you prefer the red one or the blue one?" "Should we set you up with the standard version, or would the deluxe version be better for you?"

The "order blank" close can be very persuasive as well. Basically, you fill out the order while you are presenting your products and then, when you have finished your presentation, simply hand the order form to the prospect to sign.

In all closing techniques, whoever speaks first loses. Once you ask for the order, shut up! Wait patiently with an earnest look on your face.

Sometimes it seems like it is taking hours and hours before he or she finally answers, but wait for it.

My favorite close is not conventional either. I like to use a "we" close that adds a little friendly peer pressure to the situation. "Shall we do it? OK, let's do it!"

"If you don't ask, you don't get."
                                        Stevie Wonder

Overcoming Objections

One of the most challenging aspects of a sales presentation is overcoming objections. An objection is much better than a flat no or a brush-off like, "Let me get back to you on that."

At trade shows, we often deal with the "I'll be back" brush-off. I call him mister be back. If someone says, "I'll be back" and his name isn't Arnold Schwarzenegger or Jesus Christ, there is a very real possibility you will never see him again.

Sometimes when I hear an objection, Jim Carrey's line, "So you're saying there's a chance!" comes into my head.

Objections usually arise for one of two reasons: your prospects don't completely understand why they need to purchase, or your product or service truly does not meet their needs. People usually mask these two real objections with secondary objections, such as:

- **Money**
  - o Show him or her the value, such as ROI (return on investment), savings over time, monthly payments, etc.

- **Time**
  - o Show him or her how quick and easy it will be to implement your product or service.
  - o Make it simple.

- **Just Looking**
  - o Make sure to separate yourself from your competitors.
  - o Ensure that he or she has a clear understanding of what you are presenting.
  - o Ask when he or she is looking to purchase and then ask for a follow-up appointment.

- **Too Busy**
  - o Recognize this may not be the decision maker.
  - o Ask if he or she will be less busy soon.

o Make your solution simple and not time consuming.

Sometimes you can overcome an objection with an "ego" close. I was having dinner with a leading doctor who was potentially going to place a very large order that would put my entire region over quota for the year.

Then, out of the blue, he came up with a serious objection. He didn't like the way a surgical screw seated when he placed it.

What's worse is that there was really no traditional way to counter this objection given the product we had at the time.

So I leaned over the table in his direction and said, "Do you mean to tell me that with your hands you can't make this screw work for you?"

He made the big purchase, we exceeded the annual quota, and all was well!

"Wounds from a sincere friend are better than many kisses from an enemy."

Proverbs 27:6

GETTING YOUR NEXT JOB IN SALES

Your Resume for a Sales Job

When writing a résumé for a sales position, you need to make it compelling. I have read thousands of résumés, and the vast majority were rejected by me right away.

What are the qualities of a good résumé for a position in sales, you ask? Here are some things I feel are very important:

Do not make your résumé an attendance report. Most résumés consist of where people worked, how long they worked there, their responsibilities, their educations and not much else.

In addition, make your résumé into a sales presentation that sells you. List any awards you have received, any major accomplishments you have achieved, specific details of how you have exceeded expectations, etc.

The sole purpose of your résumé is to get you an interview with the company you are hoping to work for. Make it interesting for your potential interviewer by keeping it short and strongly highlighting your accomplishments.

If your sales went from $100 to $130, it is better not to say that you had a $30 increase in sales. Instead, say you increased sales by 30%.

If your sales went from $1,000,000 to $1,050,000, it may be better to say that you increased sales by $50,000 instead of by 5%.

Do not use a form-letter version of your résumé. It will be much better if you tailor your resume to what the company is looking for in the position you are seeking.

In your "Objective," make sure to list the company by name. Do not start your "Objective" by lecturing your potential employers, as it may come across as insulting to them.

"Companies these days need . . . (*blah, blah, blah*)"

"You need to hire me because . . . (*blah, blah, blah*)"

- **Always send a cover letter.**

  o Do not use a form letter.
  o Personalize your cover letter and make sure to spell the company name correctly.

- **Let them know you researched their company and you would be honored to work for them.**

  o Mention something specific you liked from their website.

- **Provide a hard copy of your résumé.**

  o Print your résumé on nice paper.
  o Include your cover letter.
  o Put both in a nice presentation folder.

- **Call and follow up.**

  o Ask to be interviewed.

"Can you start a conversation with a total stranger? Can you take rejection? Can you accept failure and learn from your mistakes? If you answered yes to these questions, sales may just be the job for you . . ."

Pat Latunski

Interviewing for a Sales Job

When you go in to meet your interview team, you want to be well prepared. Here are some tips to help you shine in your interview:

- Thoroughly research the company's website.
  - Print out the entire website to read, study, and learn.

- Write down a short list of questions to ask the interview team.

- Look up interview questions on the Internet.
  - Print a list of anticipated interview questions and practice answering them.
  - Almost every interviewer will ask you your biggest strengths and weaknesses.
  - Practice verbalizing your answers to these questions

while looking at yourself in a mirror.

- Print at least five copies of your résumé and cover letter on nice linen paper.
  - o Buy a nice plastic folder at the office supply store for each copy.
  - o Make professional-looking personalized labels for each folder with the names of the people you know are planning to interview you.

- Bring or buy a professional-looking briefcase to put your papers in.

- Assume the sale and also bring your social security card, driver's license, references, and anything else you think you may need if they hire you on the spot.

- Look your best.
  - o Wear a new or clean and pressed conservative business suit (preferably a dark color).

- o Wear a conservative, clean, pressed shirt or top.
- o Wear new shoes or new-looking shoes with conservative socks matching your suit.

- Get a manicure the day before.
  - o Trim any excess nose and ear hair.
  - o Shave - Get a fresh haircut.
  - o Greet everyone you meet with a friendly smile and a confident handshake.

- Thank the receptionist for letting you in.

- Walk tall.

- Meeting the interview team.
  - o Do not sit down until asked.
  - o Do not complain about the weather, traffic, flight, or anything else.

- Hand out your résumé folders when appropriate.

- Answering questions.
    - o Be enthusiastic!
    - o Give short, confident answers.
    - o Look people in the eyes when you speak with them.

- Close the sale.
    - o Ask your questions.
    - o Summarize the meeting and ask for the job.

- Follow up.
    - o Follow up immediately with hand-written thank-you cards and mail them the same day.
    - o Call the person who asked you to interview and ask for the job.
        - ▪ Reinforce why you are the best candidate for the position.

"It's hard to beat someone who never gives up."

Babe Ruth

Moving Up the Ladder

At some point, most successful salespeople feel like they want to be promoted into management. After all, according to Mel Brooks in his History of the World movie, "It's good to be the king!" Right?

I feel that I am in a good position to address this topic because, in my sales career, I have been in customer service, technical service, telemarketing, inside sales, and outside sales.

I have also been an area manager, regional manager, national key account manager, national sales manager, director of global sales, director of marketing, VP of new business development, VP of sales, and VP of sales & marketing.

In most companies, the top salesperson makes more money than the sales management, and it is not entirely uncommon for him or her to make more than the VPs or even the president. So, let's look at the good, the bad, and the ugly of being promoted to the next level.

Inside Sales to Outside Sales:
This could be a logical step for you. Outside sales typically pays more, and you will have much more control over your schedule.

The downside is that your name will be on that territory and if you are unable to consistently generate enough sales to meet or exceed your territory quota, you will be fired. The fact that you are reading this book speaks volumes for you — in a good way, so go for it!

Outside Sales to Management:
Moving from outside sales to management is tricky. It takes an entirely different skillset to manage people.

Actually, in my opinion, you manage things (budgets, forecasts, and logistics) and you lead your people.

Usually you will be promoted into a middle-management position with a title something like regional manager. Your quota will become the cumulative total of all of the salespeople's quotas within the region and you will no longer have direct control over your sales.

Your job will be to grow sales in line with corporate expectations while handing down corporate edicts to your team and trying to influence upper management to get your region what you feel it needs.

Regional Management to National Management:
Remarkably, this is a fairly seamless transition. You need a similar skillset, enhanced leadership skills, larger corporate vision, and the ability to effectively interact with the other corporate management personnel.

"I went past the field of the sluggard, past the vineyard of the man who lacks judgment; thorns had come up everywhere, the ground was covered with weeds, and the stone wall was in ruins. I applied my heart to what I observed and learned a lesson from what I saw: A little

sleep, a little slumber, a little folding of the hands to rest — and poverty will come on you like a bandit and scarcity like an armed man."

Proverbs 24:30–34

Acknowledgements

This book would not be possible without the loving support of my wonderful bride, Denise Kimball Hasty. Thank you, my love.

Special thanks to my friends and family who are direct contributors and/or referred to by name in this book. Listed in alphabetical order by last name: Ashley G. Alsip, James A. Burney, Lisa Burney, Jan Fogt Casper, Melissa Endo, Dr. J. Hadley Hall, Brad Hansen, Beth Hanson, Steven Hanson, James B. Hasty, Lawrence G. Hasty, Ronald J. Hasty, Shayna Hasty, Mary Beth Heffernan, Dr. Duke Heller, Melvin Hinz, Jan Holliday, Pat Latunski, Kent Leighty, Bill Maricic, William N. Reese, Robert Regan, Bill Ryan, Fr. Joshua Wagner and Liane Holliday Willey.

I would also like to thank my other friends and family who were sources of encouragement and inspiration to me while I was writing this book. Listed in alphabetical order by last name: Frank Agin, SJ Barakony, Mayetta Barfield, Glen

Battle, Richelle Braun, Lisa Cailor, Theda Hasty Clifton, Michelle Collins, Len Conner, Lincoln Cullum, Bill Good, Gary Harper, Garry A. Hasty, Sandra Suttle Hasty, Laura Hasty-Worley, Richard Hayse, Michele Hinz, Theodore Jackson, John F. Kavanagh, Carmen Kimball, Carolyn Kimball, Chris Kimball, George Kimball, Dr. Gregori Kurtzman, Liddy Lindsey, Tina Michael-Shine, Deanna Hasty Moravec, Kelcie Moravec, Dr. Sammy Noumbissi, Lewis Post, Chris Potelicki, Angela Santelli, Terry Silberstein, Kim Smith, Drew Thornley, Jeff Wasserstrom and Rod Worley.

In addition, I would like to give a thankful shout-out to John Dougherty, DMD, at Dougherty Dental in Portland, Oregon, and Robert Heller, DDS, at Oral Implants and Reconstructive Dentistry in Lewis Center, Ohio, for your encouragement and for my smile.

Special thanks to my editor, Kate Hinz, www.katehinz.com, for making this book legible.

About the Author

Kenneth G. Hasty
Author, Speaker, Sales-Management Consultant, Sales Coach

Kenneth G. Hasty has a wealth of sales and sales-management experience spanning more than three decades. In his career, he has worked in all 50 states and several countries and achieved numerous sales awards, including "salesman of the year." He has been successful in selling situations from the open pit mines in western North America to the operating rooms of the prestigious Mayo Clinic and virtually everything in between.

Kenneth G. Hasty has held a number of national and international sales-management positions ranging from national key account manager to vice president of sales and marketing. He has been successful in most every size of company from companies ranked in the "Fortune 500" to small businesses to startup businesses.

His LinkedIn profile features well over 1,000 endorsements from his colleagues and several written recommendations as well.

Kenneth G. Hasty is available for speaking engagements, consulting, and sales training most anywhere in the world.

You can contact Kenneth G. Hasty directly at www.77secondstosales.com.

My SALES EXEC™
Sales Management & Sales Consulting
www.MySalesExec.com